A *Walking Tour of*
The University of Georgia

F. N. BONEY

A *Walking Tour of*
The University of Georgia

THE UNIVERSITY OF GEORGIA PRESS
Athens and London

© 1989 by the University of Georgia Press
Athens, Georgia 30602
All rights reserved

Printed in the United States of America

93 92 91 90 89   5 4 3 2 1

Library of Congress Cataloging in
Publication Data

Boney, F. N.
  A walking tour of the University of
Georgia / F. N. Boney.
     p. cm.
  Includes index.
  ISBN 0-8203-1081-6 (pbk.: alk. paper)
  1. University of Georgia—Description—
Guide-books. 2. University of Georgia—
History. I. Title.
LD1984.B66 1989
378.758'18—dc19   88-25997
                                        CIP

British Library Cataloging in Publication
Data available

Contents

Acknowledgments

For the bicentennial year of 1985 I published *A Pictorial History of the University of Georgia,* and this *Walking Tour* is actually a continuation of that initial effort to make our university better known. Once again the University of Georgia Press has collaborated with me. I am especially indebted to Sandra Strother Hudson, Ellen J. Harris, and Nancy Grayson Holmes for their assistance with this specialized project. Many other university organizations have helped, especially the history department, Cartographic Services Laboratory, Hargrett Rare Book and Manuscript Library, University Archives, Photographic Services, Office of Campus Planning, Athletic Association, Instructional Resources Center, and Office of Public Information. Special thanks go to photographer Walker P. Montgomery III, whose skill over the years has been vital to my efforts to tell the university's story in one way or another. Finally, I wish to thank the staff, faculty, and students at the University of Georgia for making my more than two decades on the campus a pleasant adventure.

Author's Note

The headings in this book refer to buildings used as points of reference on the tour. Adjacent buildings and landmarks discussed in the text but not named in the headings are highlighted in boldface type.

The University of Georgia

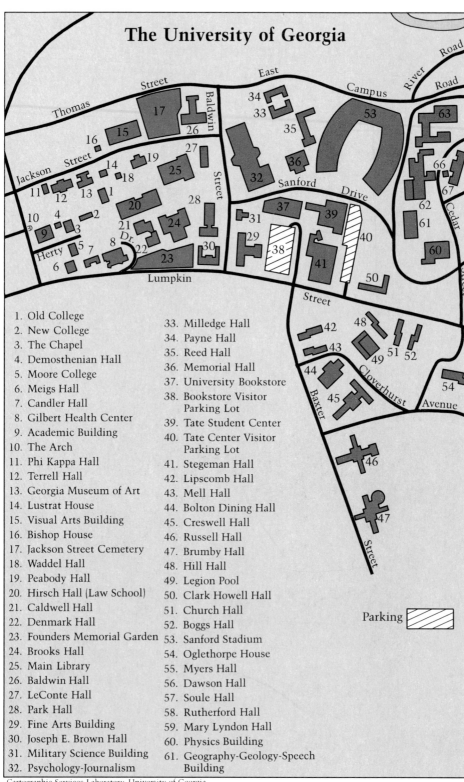

1. Old College
2. New College
3. The Chapel
4. Demosthenian Hall
5. Moore College
6. Meigs Hall
7. Candler Hall
8. Gilbert Health Center
9. Academic Building
10. The Arch
11. Phi Kappa Hall
12. Terrell Hall
13. Georgia Museum of Art
14. Lustrat House
15. Visual Arts Building
16. Bishop House
17. Jackson Street Cemetery
18. Waddel Hall
19. Peabody Hall
20. Hirsch Hall (Law School)
21. Caldwell Hall
22. Denmark Hall
23. Founders Memorial Garden
24. Brooks Hall
25. Main Library
26. Baldwin Hall
27. LeConte Hall
28. Park Hall
29. Fine Arts Building
30. Joseph E. Brown Hall
31. Military Science Building
32. Psychology-Journalism

33. Milledge Hall
34. Payne Hall
35. Reed Hall
36. Memorial Hall
37. University Bookstore
38. Bookstore Visitor Parking Lot
39. Tate Student Center
40. Tate Center Visitor Parking Lot
41. Stegeman Hall
42. Lipscomb Hall
43. Mell Hall
44. Bolton Dining Hall
45. Creswell Hall
46. Russell Hall
47. Brumby Hall
48. Hill Hall
49. Legion Pool
50. Clark Howell Hall
51. Church Hall
52. Boggs Hall
53. Sanford Stadium
54. Oglethorpe House
55. Myers Hall
56. Dawson Hall
57. Soule Hall
58. Rutherford Hall
59. Mary Lyndon Hall
60. Physics Building
61. Geography-Geology-Speech Building

Parking

Cartographic Services Laboratory, University of Georgia

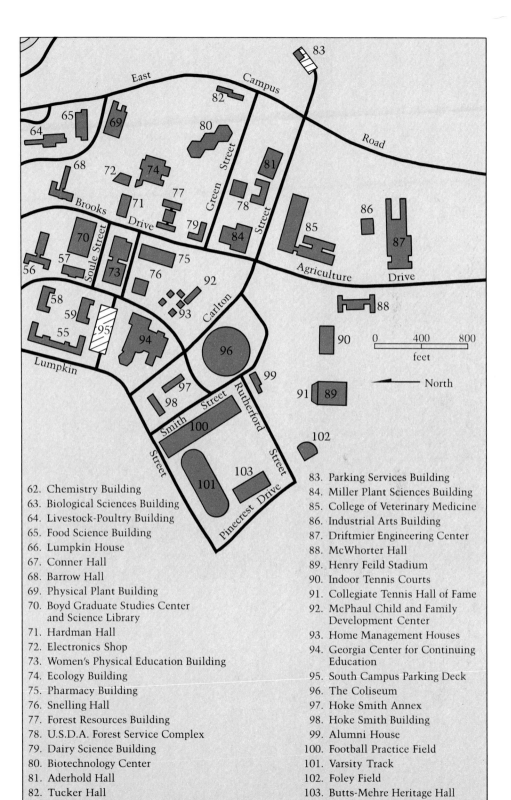

62. Chemistry Building
63. Biological Sciences Building
64. Livestock-Poultry Building
65. Food Science Building
66. Lumpkin House
67. Conner Hall
68. Barrow Hall
69. Physical Plant Building
70. Boyd Graduate Studies Center
    and Science Library
71. Hardman Hall
72. Electronics Shop
73. Women's Physical Education Building
74. Ecology Building
75. Pharmacy Building
76. Snelling Hall
77. Forest Resources Building
78. U.S.D.A. Forest Service Complex
79. Dairy Science Building
80. Biotechnology Center
81. Aderhold Hall
82. Tucker Hall

83. Parking Services Building
84. Miller Plant Sciences Building
85. College of Veterinary Medicine
86. Industrial Arts Building
87. Driftmier Engineering Center
88. McWhorter Hall
89. Henry Feild Stadium
90. Indoor Tennis Courts
91. Collegiate Tennis Hall of Fame
92. McPhaul Child and Family
    Development Center
93. Home Management Houses
94. Georgia Center for Continuing
    Education
95. South Campus Parking Deck
96. The Coliseum
97. Hoke Smith Annex
98. Hoke Smith Building
99. Alumni House
100. Football Practice Field
101. Varsity Track
102. Foley Field
103. Butts-Mehre Heritage Hall

Introduction

In 1785 the Georgia legislature chartered the nation's first state university. For the next sixteen years the University of Georgia existed only on paper; its first president, Abraham Baldwin, spent his entire term of office gathering enough money for classes to open. In 1800 the board of trustees chose a site in a remote frontier area north of Watkinsville, on a rise above the Oconee River. The next year President Josiah Meigs, Baldwin's successor, began to teach a few students in a log cabin, and by 1806 workers had completed the first permanent structure, Franklin College. The building, now known as Old College, is a copy of Connecticut Hall at Yale, the alma mater of both Baldwin and Meigs. During the next few years, several other buildings were constructed, and the town of Athens began to grow up next to the campus.

Poorly supported by the legislature, the university almost foundered after the War of 1812. Moses Waddel, a Presbyterian minister educated at Hampden-Sydney College, was appointed president in 1819, and his energy and determination kept the college alive against all odds. The task could not have been easy. In 1820 Georgia had fewer than 350,000 inhabitants: 150,000 black slaves, who were denied formal education, and 190,000 whites. No real system of public education existed; only the sons of the well-to-do could afford to study at private academies. Waddel scoured the state for qualified young men, and when he retired in 1829, Georgia had an enrollment of over a hundred students.

Waddel's successor, a Presbyterian minister named Alonzo Church, continued the previous administration's general policies for the next thirty years, as the antebellum university matured. About a hundred young men from the upper and upper middle classes studied under five professors, who presented a traditional curriculum that emphasized Latin and Greek but also required history, English, philosophy, rhetoric, science, mathematics, and a few other courses. The course of study included virtually no electives.

The campus had no organized sports or military training. The Demosthenian and Phi Kappa literary societies, the only social outlets, sponsored speeches, debates, and other activities. Almost every student belonged to one of the rival societies, and many alumni carried this commitment to the grave. The students were required to attend chapel daily and church on Sunday, and they were forbidden to have weapons, pets, whiskey, servants, or, it sometimes seemed, anything else that might threaten the stern Calvinism that permeated the campus. Many high-spirited students resisted by fighting, drinking, destroying property, and sneaking off campus at night to go to taverns or circuses. A faculty court regularly meted out punishments, and repeat offenders were sometimes expelled or "sent away."

In all of this the University of Georgia resembled other colleges, even better-known and somewhat larger universities like Yale, Virginia, and Princeton. Before the Civil War only a tiny fraction of white males could even dream of going to college, and almost all institutions of higher education, whatever their title or official status, could best be described as small, all-white, all-male, church-related, private, liberal arts colleges.

As the antebellum period ended in 1860, a Methodist minister, Andrew A. Lipscomb, became chancellor (the equivalent of president). Although the Law School was established in 1859, the outbreak of the Civil War delayed further reform for almost half a century. All over America college students put aside their books and enthusiastically marched off to the slaughter. The University of Georgia, like many other schools, soon closed for the duration.

By 1864 the tide had turned against the Confederacy. Sherman's army, on its march to the sea, passed south of Athens, by then a thriving industrial town of four thousand inhabitants. When the Confederacy collapsed in 1865, the town and the university escaped unscathed, although several college buildings were occupied briefly by a detachment of Federal troops.

The University of Georgia reopened early in 1866. Even though the campus was not damaged, the university suffered indirectly in several ways. A hundred university students and alumni had been killed in battle, and the economy of the South was in ruins. The state was destitute, so the school could not count on much direct support from the traditionally stingy legislators. However, they did pass a law that granted money for some Confederate veterans to pursue higher education, and in 1868 the university's enrollment reached three hundred for the first time. Like later veterans, these serious, mature young men did well, though most needed remedial courses. After they graduated, the university's enrollment fell sharply and did not rise to three hundred again until the end of the century.

Although Chancellor Lipscomb dreamed of reform, for many years he had to concentrate on sheer survival. Help arrived in 1872, when Georgia became a land-grant college eligible for financial support from the federal government. During the last decades of the nineteenth century, when bitterness about the war and Reconstruction was most intense in the South, "Yankee dollars" in one form or another probably kept the beleaguered university alive.

Lipscomb's successors, Henry H. Tucker, Patrick H. Mell, and William E. Boggs, continued the struggle to save the college. Like Lipscomb, these men had little opportunity to experiment; they were too busy making ends meet. Nonetheless, changes did occur. The social fraternities Sigma Alpha Epsilon, Chi Phi, Kappa Alpha,

2

and Phi Delta Theta established chapters on campus immediately after the Civil War, and others soon followed. By the end of the century fraternities had replaced the old literary societies as the main centers of student activity. The university instituted military training in the 1870s because the federal government required land-grant colleges to do so, and this, too, quickly became a regular part of college life.

In 1892 Professor Charles H. Herty introduced intercollegiate football to the campus, and student life was never quite the same again. Starting with nearby rivals like Mercer, Auburn, Georgia Tech, and the Augusta Athletic Club, the Bulldogs gradually began to play the better southern teams. During the 1920s under Coach Harry Mehre, the team scheduled games with nationally ranked squads like Harvard, Yale, Chicago, and New York University.

The last years of the nineteenth century saw other changes as well. The faculty grew to around eighteen members, a few of whom had earned the new, advanced Ph.D. degree. Several buildings were constructed. The curriculum became more diversified and less inflexible, and discipline on campus, once so strict, relaxed considerably. Though the university still had fewer than three hundred students, the population of Athens had grown to ten thousand and the state had well over two million inhabitants.

The time was ripe for the progress that occurred under Walter B. Hill, who served as chancellor from 1899 to 1905. Hill, a lawyer, was the first nonminister appointed to the post in almost a century, and the first alumnus ever to head the school. He launched the kind of sweeping reform movement that Lipscomb had dreamed of in the lean years after the Civil War. Hill moved quickly to tranform a small liberal arts college educating a chosen few into a major state university committed to serving all of the people of Georgia. He coaxed much larger appropriations out of the state legislature, rallied the alumni to more active support, increased enrollment, expanded the curriculum and the faculty, developed a summer school to improve teacher training, and supported graduate education. He also undertook many construction projects on the campus, which had grown very little since the Civil War.

Most important of all, he tried to justify federal support by establishing for the first time a vigorous college of agriculture. The new models for the university were midwestern land-grant colleges like the University of Wisconsin, which Hill visited to observe and to learn.

Although Hill died after only six years in office, the momentum he created carried over into the administration of his successor, David C. Barrow, a graduate of the class of 1874 who had served as dean under Hill. In 1907 Barrow hired Andrew M. Soule to direct the agricultural expansion. From Conner Hall on the new south campus, Soule provided vigorous leadership for the agricultural college for twenty-five years.

The most decisive event of Barrow's tenure was the admission of undergraduate women in 1918. For many years afterward, women remained a minority concentrated in traditional women's fields like education and home economics. Still, their presence broke one of the last barriers to modernization as Georgia moved into the twentieth century.

Lively parties and powerful football teams became part of the Georgia image, but the school continued to make academic progress. Enrollment, pushed over a thousand for the first time by the admission of women, almost reached two thousand by the end of the 1920s and exceeded three thousand during the depression of the 1930s, when federal relief funds financed the construction of seventeen new buildings.

In 1932 the Board of Regents of the University System of Georgia was established as part of the reorganization of state government under Governor Richard B. Russell (class of 1918). The regents exercised control over the entire state system of higher education, including the University of Georgia. Because most of them were graduates of Georgia, the university received at least a fair share of the limited funds available for higher education during the depression.

Early in 1941 Governor Eugene Talmadge (class of 1908) dealt the university a stunning blow. Intervening directly in campus affairs, he forced the dismissal of several faculty members who were rumored to be sympathetic to racial integration. President Harmon Caldwell (class of 1919) protested Talmadge's interference vigorously, but to no avail. The Southern Association of Colleges and Secondary Schools withdrew accreditation from the university and all the other white schools in the system. Fortunately for the university, Talmadge was repudiated in the gubernatorial election of 1942, and the new governor, Ellis G. Arnall (class of 1931), acted quickly to restore accreditation.

World War II presented President Caldwell with many other challenges. Enrollment plummeted as the draft mobilized millions of young men for battle, and for the first time in the university's history women made up the majority of undergraduates. A naval preflight program brought a constant flow of new trainees to the campus, but these men in their regimented, accelerated program had almost no contact with regular undergraduates.

When the war ended in 1945, a flood of veterans returned to complete or begin their educations, and enrollment expanded temporarily to almost eight thousand. Many students were older than the traditional age, and many were married. During the postwar period women undergraduates again became the minority and remained so until the 1970s.

In 1948 Caldwell was appointed chancellor of the entire University System. Omer Clyde Aderhold (class of 1923), who was named president of the university in 1950, led a highly successful administration that lasted seventeen years. Under Aderhold the curriculum was broadened and deepened, and graduate studies grew rapidly. The faculty, who were increasingly better educated, turned more of their energies toward research and publication. The sciences in particular flourished on the newer south campus, especially after the construction of the Science Center in 1959–60.

The last great barrier to modernization fell in 1961, when the university was integrated. The arrival of the first two black students on campus was greeted with an uneasy calm, but several days later a riot flared after a basketball game. The mob was dispersed by university officials and Athens police, and both students remained in school and later graduated. Slowly the university proceeded with the task of integrating blacks and whites on a traditional southern campus.

An important factor in the health of the university was the state's economy, which had boomed since World War II. For the first time, enough funds were available from state, federal, and private sources to support the transformation of the school into a first-rate modern university. By the time Aderhold retired in 1967, the student body numbered over sixteen thousand—more than twice as large as it had been at the beginning of his tenure.

Aderhold's successor was Fred C. Davison (class of 1952), who led the university for nineteen years of unprecedented growth, during which enrollment soared to twenty-six thousand and the number of faculty approached two thousand. The student disruptions of the late 1960s and early 1970s had only limited effect on the conservative Georgia campus, but student protests did force the university to relinquish its power as parent

away from home. The students, especially women, gained much greater freedom on and off campus. Partly as a result of the relaxation of residence rules, the university has constructed no new dormitories since 1970, and many more students now live off campus, strengthening town-gown connections.

The theme of the 1980s has been an increasing stress on graduate training, off-campus service, and research and publication. The emphasis on science and technology has continued, recently focusing on the emerging interdisciplinary field of biotechnology.

Explosive growth in recent decades has created an almost new university in Athens, but the modern school is the direct descendant of the tiny college that struggled for its existence in the early nineteenth century. Like other colleges, Georgia has traveled its own special road toward becoming a great university. Now, under its twentieth president, Charles B. Knapp, the University of Georgia moves confidently ahead.

For more detailed information about the University of Georgia, see F. N. Boney, *A Pictorial History of the University of Georgia* (Athens: University of Georgia Press, 1984); and Thomas G. Dyer, *The University of Georgia: A Bicentennial History, 1785–1985* (Athens: University of Georgia Press, 1985).

North Campus

North Campus

1. Old College
2. New College
3. The Chapel
4. Demosthenian Hall
5. Moore College
6. Meigs Hall
7. Candler Hall
8. Gilbert Health Center
9. Academic Building
10. The Arch
11. Phi Kappa Hall
12. Terrell Hall
13. Georgia Museum of Art
14. Lustrat House
15. Visual Arts Building
16. Bishop House
17. Jackson Street Cemetery
18. Waddel Hall
19. Peabody Hall
20. Hirsch Hall (Law School)
21. Caldwell Hall
22. Denmark Hall
23. Founders Memorial Garden
24. Brooks Hall
25. Main Library
26. Baldwin Hall
27. LeConte Hall
28. Park Hall
29. Fine Arts Building
30. Joseph E. Brown Hall
31. Military Science Building
32. Psychology-Journalism
33. Milledge Hall
34. Payne Hall
35. Reed Hall
36. Memorial Hall
37. University Bookstore
38. Bookstore Visitor Parking Lot
39. Tate Student Center
40. Tate Center Visitor Parking Lot
41. Stegeman Hall
42. Lipscomb Hall
43. Mell Hall
44. Bolton Dining Hall
45. Creswell Hall
46. Russell Hall
47. Brumby Hall
48. Hill Hall
49. Legion Pool
50. Clark Howell Hall
51. Church Hall
52. Boggs Hall
53. Sanford Stadium

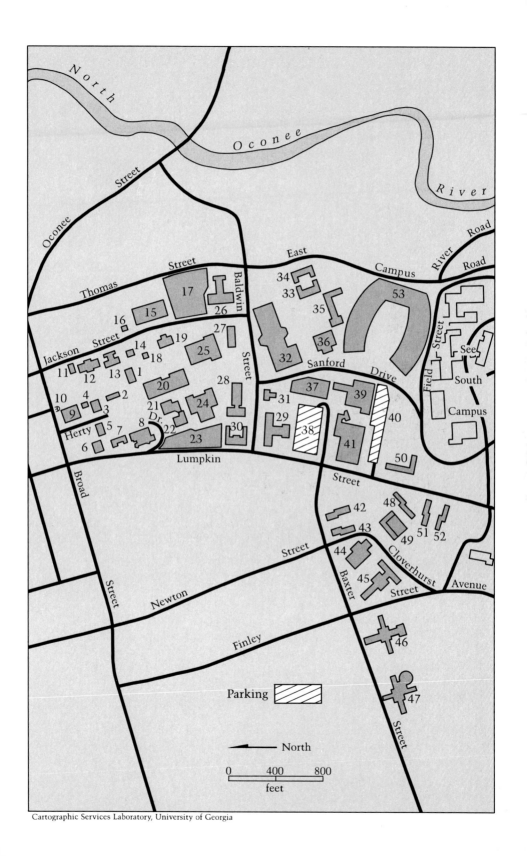

North

Oconee

Street

Oconee

Street

Street

R i v e r

River Road

Road

East

Campus

Thomas

Baldwin

17

26

34

33

35

53

15

16

Jackson   Street

14   19

18

27

25

Street

Field Street

See

South

32

36

Sanford

Drive

Campus

11

12   13   1

10   4   2

9   3

20

28

37

39

40

21

24

31

38

41

Herty   5   7   8

Dr.

6

22   23   30

29

50

Lumpkin

Street

Broad

42

48

43

51   52

49

Street

44

Baxter

45

Cloverhurst

Street

Avenue

Newton

Street

Finley

46

Parking

47

North

Street

0   400   800

feet

Cartographic Services Laboratory, University of Georgia

Old College

1806

Let's begin at the beginning. Old College, completed in 1806, was the first permanent building on the campus and is the oldest surviving structure in this part of Georgia. Modeled after Connecticut Hall at Yale, Old College was constructed as an all-purpose building but soon was used mainly as a dormitory. The building was originally called Franklin College; during much of the nineteenth century the name was often applied to the university itself, even though the official name of the school has always been the University of Georgia.

Alexander H. Stephens, vice-president of the Confederacy, and Crawford W. Long, a pioneer in the use of anesthesia, shared a room in Old College when they were students in 1832. The room is marked by a plaque on the northwestern corner of the second floor. In front of the north side of the building stands a large marker honoring Abraham Baldwin, the father of the University of Georgia. Baldwin, a native of Connecticut, was a Yale graduate and a veteran of the Revolutionary War. In 1785, while a member of the state legislature, he wrote the charter of the university. Although Baldwin is officially the first president of the institution, he spent his entire term of office trying to collect enough money for the university to open its doors. By the time classes actually began in 1801, he was representing Georgia in the U.S. Senate and therefore resigned the presidency in favor of his friend and protégé Josiah Meigs. Baldwin remained in the Senate until his death in 1807.

By the beginning of the twentieth century, Old College, often derisively called "Yahoo Hall," had deteriorated so badly that it had been boarded up, and Chancellor Hill planned to demolish it. In 1908 supporters campaigning to preserve the historic building collected ten thousand dollars to pay for its restoration. A new brick surface replaced the crumbling exterior, and students returned to its antique rooms.

During World War II the United States Navy, which selected the University of Georgia as the site of a preflight training program, thoroughly redesigned and reconstructed the interior for use as "Yorktown Barracks." Today the building is occupied by administrative offices. Old College also houses the Institute of Community and Area Development, which provides research and consultation services to regional planning commissions, state agencies, and local governments.

On the south side of the building is the President's Club Garden. On a low brick wall in the garden is a list of the names of persons who have made major financial contributions to the university.

Old College and the other buildings that date from the antebellum campus are listed in the National Register of Historic Places.

New College

1823

New College was constructed in 1823 as a dormitory, library, and classroom building. The original four-story structure burned to the ground in 1830. Although no lives were lost, the library and a great deal of equipment vanished in the flames. Rebuilt in 1832 without the fourth floor, New College then closely resembled nearby Old College.

Over the years New College, though designed primarily as a dormitory, has served many purposes. Early in the twentieth century a snack bar (the Co-op) and the college bookstore occupied the first floor. After World War II the pharmacy department took over the entire building. Since the 1960s it has housed the office of the dean of the Franklin College of Arts and Sciences and various other administrative units.

The Chapel

1832

Built in 1832 to replace a temporary wooden structure, the Chapel is one of the most aesthetically pleasing buildings at Georgia. At the time of its construction, at a cost of fifteen thousand dollars, it was the finest building on campus. In the early days, when Protestant orthodoxy dominated the campus, the Chapel was a center of campus activities. A daily religious service, which students were required to attend, was held there, as were assemblies and commencements.

A bell tower originally crowned the roof, but in 1913 it was found to be rotten and was removed. The bell, which rang for chapel, for the beginning and end of class, and in emergencies, was placed at the top of a wooden tower at the back of the Chapel. Now the bell is rung only to mark athletic victories or other special occasions.

Inside the building hangs a 17-by-23½-foot painting by George Cooke of the interior of Saint Peter's in Rome. The painting was presented to the school in 1867 by the Alabama industrialist Daniel Pratt. In 1955 it was badly damaged by fire. Local artist Walter Frobos and his daughter spent eighteen months restoring the painting, mounting it on masonite, and framing it in redwood.

The sundial in front of the Chapel marks the site of the famous Toombs Oak. A famous senator and Confederate general, Robert Toombs began his distinguished career by being expelled from the university in 1825. As the story goes, he reappeared at commencement and spoke so eloquently under the oak tree that the audience left the Chapel to hear him. The incident, first recounted in a speech by Henry W. Grady (class of 1868), sounds just like the mercurial, impetuous Toombs—but, alas, it never happened. Toombs's love for the university did cause him to return many times to the campus, however, and he served on the board of trustees from 1859 until his death in 1885.

Today the Chapel is used primarily as a recital hall for the School of Music. Lectures, meetings, and other small gatherings also are held there.

Demosthenian Hall

1824

Literary and debating societies played a major role at antebellum colleges like Georgia. The Demosthenian Literary Society was founded in 1803, and in 1824 Demosthenian Hall was constructed at a cost of four thousand dollars. Demosthenian—an example of the federal style, with a Palladian window over the entrance—and the Chapel are the two really fine early buildings on the campus.

In 1979–81 the Demosthenian Society restored the lower floor of the building. The upper floor, which has always been used as a meeting room, remains much as it was in the early days, when many long, heated debates and discussions were held there. Although the Demosthenians are few in number now, they maintain all of the old traditions. The building is open to the public only on special occasions, but informal visits are possible if members of the society are present.

Moore College

1874

Only one permanent structure appeared on campus during the lean period from the end of the Civil War to the beginning of the twentieth century. In the absence of financial support from the state legislature, Richard Moore, an Athens physician and a member of the university's board of trustees, persuaded the city of Athens to appropriate the necessary twenty-five thousand dollars for a new classroom building. Professor Leon Henri Charbonnier, a graduate of the French military school at St. Cyr and a professor of mathematics and engineering at Georgia for almost forty years, designed Moore College. It was completed in 1874 on a site immediately behind the Chapel. Marked by a distinctive mansard roof, Moore is the only French Second Empire building on campus.

The cadet corps, established after Georgia became a land-grant college in 1872, drilled just south of Moore College, on a field that is now a large parking lot. From 1892 to 1911 the area was used as the main athletic field. Here all of the early intercollegiate football and baseball games were played, and here a wild riot erupted in 1893 after the first football game with Georgia Tech. The victorious Tech team barely managed to get out of town, and the fierce rivalry has continued unabated for almost a century.

Moore College originally provided space for the technical and scientific classes that were offered to fulfill Georgia's new role as a federal land-grant college. It continued to house the Department of Physics until the new Science Center opened on the south campus in the late 1950s. The Department of Romance Languages now occupies the building.

Meigs Hall · Candler Hall

1905 · 1902

Meigs Hall

This rather plain building just to the north of Moore College was originally called LeConte Hall. It was later renamed Meigs Hall in honor of Josiah Meigs, second president of the university. Meigs, a New Englander, was in a sense the first real head of the college: Abraham Baldwin, the first president, resigned before the university actually opened its doors in 1801. Meigs patterned the new school after his alma mater, Yale. Like his friend Thomas Jefferson, he was greatly interested in the sciences and gave them a little more emphasis than was customary in those early years, when most colleges followed a rather rigid classical curriculum.

Although the university was poorly supported by the legislature, Meigs managed to keep the college open, and enrollment grew steadily toward a hundred. In 1810, however, after a bitter dispute with the board of trustees, Meigs resigned and returned to the North, where he died in 1822.

Meigs Hall was built during the administration of Walter B. Hill. Now occupied by the Department of Germanic and Slavic Languages, it was designed to accommodate classes in the sciences, which Chancellor Hill wished to strengthen in order to balance the university's traditional emphasis on the liberal arts. South of Meigs Hall stands Candler Hall, which was named for Governor Allen D. Candler. Originally a dormitory, Candler now houses the Institute of Higher Education, the Office of International Development, and offices and classrooms for several other departments. South of Candler Hall is the **Gilbert Health Center**, a complex of buildings constructed in the 1940s and the 1970s. The center, which houses an infirmary and various other health services for students, is named for Judge Price Gilbert, a generous benefactor of the university. To the west, across Lumpkin Street, are several fraternity houses.

Candler Hall

Academic Building

1905

Although the Academic Building is usually dated 1905, it is actually an antebellum building—or rather, two antebellum buildings. In 1831 a two-story classroom and library building was constructed just north of Demosthenian Hall. The structure was soon called the Ivy Building because of the tangle of green foliage that covered the front. To the north, between the Ivy Building and Broad Street, stood a wooden Presbyterian church built during the administration of Moses Waddel (1819–29).

In 1862 the church was demolished to make way for a new, larger library building. The college's small collection of books was easily housed on the second floor of the Library Building, the third floor held a museum of natural history, and on the first floor was a lecture hall that could accommodate three hundred people. Sarah Frierson, the first woman on the staff of the university, was librarian from 1888 until she retired in 1910.

At the turn of the century, Professor Charles N. Strahan (class of 1883), who taught civil engineering and mathematics on campus for sixty-two years, formed a plan to unite the two old structures. In 1905 he directed the expansion of the Ivy Building, which he then connected to the Library Building by constructing between the two buildings a large Corinthian portico in the front and rooms across the back.

Like most of the other old buildings, Academic has served many functions over the years but is now occupied by administrative offices. As late as the end of World War II, the first floor provided office space for the entire university administration, and the top two floors were devoted to classrooms. This hybrid structure now houses various offices under the Vice President for Student Affairs: Financial Aid, Admissions, Judicial Programs, Honors Program, and the Registrar's Office. The latter maintains records of students' grades, transcripts, and enrollment certification.

The Arch

1858

Late in the antebellum period the university sold its nearby botanical garden for a thousand dollars and used the money to erect a new iron fence along Broad Street. The main entrance to the campus was the Arch, modeled after the great seal of the state. The Arch originally could be closed by two iron gates, which soon disappeared. Over the generations the Arch became one of the primary symbols of the university; until recent years freshmen were forbidden to walk beneath it.

The Arch has always been the main gateway between the university and Athens, which now has a metropolitan population of over 150,000. The downtown business district, the oldest part of the city, lies directly across Broad Street from the iron fence. Beside the Arch stands a state historical marker that proclaims Georgia the first chartered state university in America.

Phi Kappa Hall

1836

Walking east along the iron fence, the visitor crosses an open area which early in the twentieth century contained four tennis courts. The first building on the east side of the quadrangle is the home of the Phi Kappa Literary Society, organized in 1820 to compete with the Demosthenians. This rather plain classical structure, which faces Demosthenian Hall across the quadrangle, was not built until 1836. Immediately after the Civil War, Union troops briefly occupied this building, using the ground floor as a stable and the top floor for parties; but they were probably not much more destructive than the rambunctious antebellum students had been.

The coming of social fraternities, intercollegiate athletics, and other distractions during the late nineteenth and early twentieth centuries gradually weakened both literary societies. The Demosthenians survived, but World War II provided the *coup de grâce* for Phi Kappa, and recent efforts to revive the society have failed.

For many years the late E. Merton Coulter used the ground floor for his office and large personal library, which now belongs to the university library. Coulter taught history at the university from 1919 to 1958. A prolific scholar even in retirement, he served as editor of the *Georgia Historical Quarterly* for fifty years before his death in 1981. Coulter's *College Life in the Old South* (1925) is a lively account of day-to-day activities at the University of Georgia from its beginning until 1870.

The ground floor of Phi Kappa Hall

is now used as a computer training center. The upper floor is usually locked for security reasons. Like the upper floor of Demosthenian Hall, it is still furnished as a meeting place, much as it was in the days when students gathered to sharpen their wits and find escape from the direct control of the faculty. Quiet, almost eerie, it is one of the few spots in the modern university where the antebellum college still seems to live.

Terrell Hall

1904

Even before Chancellor Hill took office in 1899, the university had begun to outgrow its original mold as a small liberal-arts college. In 1896 the legislature appropriated enough money for a large new building, and the following year a three-story brick structure with a cupola was erected to the south of Phi Kappa Hall. Hill named it Science Hall and made it the focal point of his efforts to stimulate science and technical training at the university.

Six years later the grand new building burned to the ground, but Hill quickly replaced it with Terrell Hall, named in honor of William Terrell, an antebellum planter who had endowed a chair of agriculture at the university. Terrell Hall was built on the foundation of Science Hall; at the northwestern corner one can still see the original cornerstone, dated 1897. A Renaissance Revival structure, designed by Professor Charles Strahan, Terrell Hall has never won aesthetic acclaim. Nonetheless, it is of architectural significance because it confirmed the tendency to avoid any set architectural pattern on the campus.

For many years Terrell housed the pharmacy department. Today the University of Georgia Press occupies the ground floor; the Press, founded in 1938, publishes approximately seventy-five books a year for the benefit of scholars and educated laypersons. The Office of Public Information and the Carl Vinson Institute of Government are upstairs.

Georgia Museum of Art

1905

The early university never had an adequate library; in the antebellum period the two literary societies had as many books as the college library. Early in the twentieth century, George Foster Peabody gave sixty thousand dollars for a new neoclassical building that could house enough books to meet the university's needs. A native of Columbus, Georgia, Peabody moved to New York City with his parents after the Civil War. Starting from scratch with a very limited education, he made a fortune in banking. When he first visited the Georgia campus in 1901, Chancellor Hill enlisted his support. Peabody, a philanthropist in the mold of Andrew Carnegie, gave generously to many worthy causes, and over the years the university benefited handsomely. Peabody is probably the greatest benefactor in the university's history.

The library's resources began to grow slowly but surely. Although the new building was designed specifically to accommodate books and readers, it naturally served other purposes as well. One professor complained that students were wasting time there, instead of studying. After the admission of women in 1918, he lamented that "would-be lovers" came there only to "jelly."

In 1953 the library, which had outgrown its quarters once again, was moved to a much larger building farther south on the old campus. The structure that Peabody built now houses the Georgia Museum of Art, which was established in 1945, when Alfred H. Holbrook donated his collection of American paintings to the university. The collection has grown steadily to more than five thousand works of art, including Italian Renaissance and American paintings and many prints and drawings by American, European, and oriental masters. The museum displays traveling exhibitions as well as its own holdings, and schedules many lectures and films.

In 1982 the Georgia General Assembly designated the Georgia Museum of Art as the state's official art museum. A much larger museum building is on the drawing boards, and the present building will eventually serve the university in some other capacity. The Museum is open to the public from 9 A.M. to 5 P.M. Monday through Saturday and from 1 to 5 P.M. on Sunday.

Lustrat House

1847

Lustrat, an antebellum faculty house, was built some yards north of its present site but was moved in 1905 to make way for the new library, now the Georgia Museum of Art. It is named for Joseph Lustrat, a native of Paris who succeeded Leon Henri Charbonnier in 1898. Lustrat, who was for many years head of the De-partment of Romance Languages, lived here with his wife and three daughters until his death in 1927. For some years afterward, Mrs. Lustrat continued to live in the house, renting rooms to students. Lustrat House, one of two surviving faculty houses on campus, is now the office of the president of the university.

Visual Arts Building

1961

Behind Lustrat House, across Jackson Street, is the modernistic Visual Arts Building, which houses the Department of Art. The well-known painter Lamar Dodd established the department in 1938 and served as its head until his retirement in 1973. The department has flourished and now offers a full range of courses with emphasis on graphic design, photographic design, and printmaking. The department also sponsors a summer program in Cortona, Italy. During the week, when the Visual Arts Building is open for classes, visitors are welcome to walk through the main gallery, where students display their work.

Just to the north of the building is **Bishop House**, originally a town residence constructed in 1837. For many years, until the completion of the Park Hall Annex in 1970, the Depart-

ment of Classics occupied the small house. It now provides additional space for the Department of Art.

On the south side of the Visual Arts Building lies the **Jackson Street Cemetery**, the first burial ground in the area. The cemetery was part of the original university land grant, and students who died at school were buried there, as were many townspeople. After the railroad reached Athens in 1841, the bodies of students were sent home for burial. Gradually the boundaries of the graveyard shrank, until today they encompass only two and a half acres. Because this small spot is near the center of campus, the university has made several attempts to build there. Each time, however, public opinion has prevented the destruction of the cemetery, and today the Old Athens Cemetery Foundation maintains and preserves it.

Waddel Hall

1821

Immediately to the south of Lustrat House is Waddel Hall, completed in 1821. Waddel is older than any campus building except Old College, and it was built in the federal style, austere and unpretentious. It was originally known as Philosophical Hall because it housed books and equipment for the sciences, then called "natural philosophy." In the 1950s it was renamed Waddel Hall in honor of Moses Waddel, president of the university from 1819 to 1829.

Like many of the old buildings on campus, Waddel has served many purposes. It has been a classroom building, a gymnasium, and a boardinghouse. In the 1870s the agricultural college moved into the building, which is one of the smallest on campus. For most of the first half of the twentieth century it was the home of Thomas W. Reed, the well-known registrar of the university. The offices of the University of Georgia Press were in Waddel Hall until 1977, when the building was renovated to accommodate the Dean Rusk Center for International and Comparative Law.

George Peabody Hall

1913

The University of Georgia has had two benefactors named George Peabody. George Foster Peabody was a native of Columbus who gave generously to the university in the early twentieth century. Peabody Hall, however, is named for an earlier George Peabody, a New England merchant who made a fortune in transatlantic trade. Peabody, who died in 1869, directed in his will that his estate be distributed over a period of time to promote public education in the South.

In the early twentieth century the University of Georgia received forty thousand dollars from Peabody's estate. The university used the funds to construct a building for the School of Education, which moved into the new quarters in 1913. The admission of women to the university in 1918 caused a rapid growth in education enrollment, however, and the program outgrew the space within two decades. Peabody Hall now houses the Departments of Philosophy and Religion.

Hirsch Hall

1932

When the School of Law was established in 1859, classes met in the law office of T. R. R. Cobb and Joseph Henry Lumpkin, four blocks northwest of the campus. For many years the curriculum consisted of one year of study beyond high school. The faculty was small: Cobb and William Hope Hull taught regularly, and Lumpkin lectured in his spare time. Although until recent years the School of Law was little known beyond the Southeast, most Georgia governors have been alumni (Lester Maddox and Jimmy Carter are two recent exceptions). By the 1920s two years of undergraduate college work were required for admission. The school then had five professors and about 120 students, squeezed into inadequate quarters on the north side of Broad Street.

Recognizing that the school could not continue to grow in such conditions, alumni raised eighty thousand dollars to construct a new building directly across the quadrangle from Peabody Hall. Harold Hirsch Hall, completed in 1932, was named for a member of the class of 1901, the general counsel and vice-president of Coca-Cola, who was a generous benefactor of the Law School.

The opening of Hirsch Hall marked the beginning of a new era. The School of Law soon received full national accreditation, and its growth has continued. Today the law faculty numbers about forty members, who teach approximately six hundred students. In 1967 and 1981 the school constructed large modernistic additions to the classical Hirsch Hall.

Caldwell Hall · Denmark Hall

1981 · 1901

Caldwell Hall

Immediately behind the Law School stands Caldwell Hall, which is tucked so closely among earlier structures that it is easily missed in spite of its size. It is the only major building on the original campus that is still primarily devoted to classroom teaching, though it also houses the administrative offices of the School of Environmental Design.

Caldwell Hall is named for Harmon W. Caldwell, who received an A.B. degree from the University of Georgia in 1919 and then earned a law degree at Harvard. He began to teach at the Law School in 1929 and became its dean in 1933, soon after the opening of Hirsch Hall. Two years later he began a thirteen-year tenure as president of the University of Georgia. During Caldwell's administration the university's enrollment grew from a little over two thousand to almost eight thousand, and he instituted the first major program of campus landscaping and beautification. More important, he laid the foundations for Georgia's progress toward becoming a major research institution, though he lacked the funds to stimulate the kind of expansion that came in the 1960s.

West of Caldwell Hall is a small building named for Brantley A. Denmark, class of 1871, who led several major alumni fund drives. Denmark Hall was constructed in 1901 as the campus dining hall, with a small infirmary on the second floor. The students called it the "Beanery" and called the food all sorts of things, though the meals were adequate and inexpensive—a good bargain. The building, remodeled in the 1950s, is now used primarily for the graduate program of the School of Environmental Design.

Founders Memorial Garden

1940

In 1891 the first garden club in America was organized in Athens. In 1939, the Garden Clubs of Georgia and the university's Department of Landscape Architecture agreed to cooperate in establishing a garden in honor of the founding members. The garden, designed by Professor Hubert B. Owens, later dean of the School of Environmental Design, is a quiet refuge in the midst of the hustle and bustle of the contemporary campus. The adjoining faculty house (1857) has been restored and furnished as a museum, which is also the headquarters of the Garden Club of Georgia.

Brooks Hall

1928

The Commerce-Journalism Building, completed in 1928, is a balanced, classical structure designed by the distinguished architect Neel Reid. As the original name implies, the Departments of Commerce and Journalism were quartered there, and the Department of Romance Languages occupied part of the building for a time.

In 1961 the building was named in honor of Robert Preston Brooks, class of 1904. Brooks, the university's first Rhodes scholar, received a Ph.D. from the University of Wisconsin in 1912 and returned to the University of Georgia to teach history. In 1920 he became dean of the School of Commerce, a post that he held for twenty-five years. During his tenure the school, now known as the College of Business Administration, grew steadily. Although a sizeable addition was constructed in 1972, Brooks Hall is barely able to meet the growing demand for courses in business.

Library

1953

In 1944 Ilah Dunlap Little bequeathed four hundred thousand dollars to the university for the construction of a new library, on two conditions: the building must have columns on all sides, and it was to be built on the site of the Chancellor's House, an antebellum brick structure. At the time, although the existing library building was too small, the university lacked the additional funds necessary to begin construction. Soon after O. C. Aderhold became president in 1950, the legislature appropriated additional funds, and the Chancellor's House was demolished to clear the site. The building, completed in 1953 at a total cost of two million dollars, has true columns only on the front; the other columns are false, to save money.

During the 1960s the library's holdings, which had numbered three hundred thousand volumes in 1950, grew so rapidly that books were shelved in every crevice. In 1974 an annex, far larger than the original building, was constructed at the back. Today the university's combined libraries—the Main Library and the Law Library on the north campus, and the Science Library on the south campus—hold over 2.6 million books, serials, and documents. An elaborate computer system, rapidly expanding to encompass the entire collection, catalogs and keeps up with the mass of material.

The Hargrett Rare Book and Manuscript Library, on the third floor of the Main Library, contains a wealth of Georgia material and many Confederate documents, including the original handwritten Confederate Constitution of 1861. In the basement is the Richard B. Russell Memorial

Library, which contains the papers of Senator Russell (class of 1918), Senator Herman Talmadge (class of 1936), and Dean Rusk, former United States secretary of state. The basement also houses a very large microfilm collection of special use to historians and genealogists.

Although a university identification card is normally required to check materials out of the libraries, members of the public are welcome to use most resources of the library within the building. The libraries also cooperate in the interlibrary loan program.

The offices of the *Georgia Review*, a journal of arts and letters published by the university since 1947, are on the second floor of the Main Library. The *Review* publishes essays, poetry, fiction, and book reviews of interest to the informed nonspecialist reader.

Baldwin, LeConte, and Park Halls

1938

Baldwin Hall

Behind the Main Library stand three similar buildings, all constructed during the depression by the Public Works Administration, as part of President Roosevelt's New Deal. Buildings in the same style can be found on many other campuses all over the nation.

Baldwin Hall, east of the Library on the other side of Jackson Street, was built for the College of Education. It now provides office and classroom space for the Departments of Sociology, Political Science, and Anthropology. The Center for Global Policy Studies and the Criminal Justice Program are also housed there. The building is named for Abraham Baldwin, the author of the university's charter and the first president of the college.

Immediately behind the Library is LeConte Hall, named for Joseph LeConte, class of 1841, who became a distinguished science professor at the university in the 1850s. After the Civil War, LeConte helped to establish the University of California at Berkeley. LeConte Hall was designed for the biological sciences, but the Department of History has occupied the building for many years.

West of LeConte stands Park Hall, named for Robert Emory Park, head of the Department of English from 1900 until his death in 1942. The Departments of English, Classics, and Comparative Literature are housed in the main building and in an annex built in 1970.

LeConte Hall

Park Hall

Fine Arts Building · Joseph E. Brown Hall

1941 · 1932

Fine Arts Building

Across the street from the Park Hall Annex is the Fine Arts Building, completed just before the United States entered World War II. Fine Arts, which houses the School of Music and the Department of Drama, contains classrooms, offices, practice rooms, and several small theaters. At the center of the building is the Fine Arts Theater, which has a seating capacity of 750. The theater is used for concerts, plays, and other cultural events.

The performing arts programs have long since outgrown the Fine Arts Building, designed to serve a student body of 3,600. To relieve the crowded conditions in Fine Arts, the School of Music and the Department of Drama also share Joseph E. Brown Hall, directly across the street. Joe Brown Hall, named for Georgia's Civil War governor, was built in 1932 as a dormitory. Most of the rooms are small and are therefore used as faculty and administrative offices.

Immediately east of the Fine Arts Building stands the **Military Science Building** (1931), which houses the Army R.O.T.C. program.

Psychology-Journalism Complex

1968

Directly across Baldwin Street from LeConte Hall is the Psychology-Journalism Complex, built in 1968. The taller building to the east houses the Department of Psychology; on the west side is the School of Journalism and Mass Communication, which administers the well-known George F. Peabody Awards, given each spring to outstanding performers in radio and television. On the plaza between the two buildings are two auditoriums, each seating more than three hundred.

The complex occupies the site of the old varsity tennis courts and Woodruff Hall, a dilapidated gym-nasium where home basketball games were played until the Coliseum was completed in 1964.

Southeast of the complex are three dormitories: **Milledge Hall** (1925), named for Governor John Milledge, who helped select the site of the university and donated the original 633 acres; **Payne Hall** (1940), named for Professor William Oscar Payne, who served as faculty chairman of athletics for many years; and **Reed Hall** (1953), named for Registrar Thomas E. ("Uncle Tom") Reed, class of 1888, who was a university administrator for almost forty years.

Memorial Hall

1925

After a lengthy fund drive and several construction delays, Memorial Hall was completed in 1925 to honor the forty-seven University of Georgia men who died in World War I. The building was an expansion of Alumni Hall, a one-story structure that contained a swimming pool and gymnasium.

Since its completion, Memorial Hall has always provided space for a variety of student activities: it had a ballroom and a billiard room, and for years the small campus bookstore was located on the main floor. In the 1930s some of the first foreign students at the university lived in small rooms tucked under the sloping roof. In those days before air conditioning, they must have received a memorable introduction to southern summers.

The U.S. Navy enlarged the building during World War II.

Although the bookstore and the student center have moved to larger quarters across the street, Memorial Hall remains important in campus life. During the university's bicentennial, the main floor furnished space for a museum tracing the development of the university since its charter was signed in 1785; now it contains a faculty dining room. The registration center for the entire campus occupies the main floor of Memorial Hall. The central location is more convenient for the students, who are busily engaged getting papers and forms stamped, signed, stapled, and occasionally rejected as part of the quarterly registration ritual.

University Bookstore

1968

Over the years the bookstore has been given space in many different buildings—Waddel Hall, New College, Phi Kappa Hall, and Memorial Hall. In 1968, when more than sixteen thousand students were enrolled, the university built a modern bookstore in a convenient central location, and in 1987 a massive expansion almost doubled the floor space. The university now boasts a splendid facility. Even so, at the beginning of each new academic session the flood of students buying new books and other supplies taxes the bookstore to its limits. Home football games at Sanford Stadium produce another tidal wave of customers, who buy large numbers of T-shirts, bumper stickers, banners, and all sorts of other Bulldog paraphernalia as well as books.

Tate Student Center

1983

A covered walkway connects the Bookstore with the Tate Student Center. This ultramodern structure, completed in 1983, offers a variety of services and facilities. The main floor contains a cafeteria, a game room, a movie theater seating five hundred, and various administrative offices. Downstairs are a large television room and an equipment rental room. On the ground floor are a post office, a photocopying service, banquet rooms, and numerous meeting rooms.

The Tate Center is named for William Tate (A.B., 1924; M.A., 1927), who joined the faculty of his alma mater in 1936 as an instructor of English and dean of freshmen. During his twenty-five years as dean of men, Tate became a campus institution. He enforced the university's social and academic rules with a mixture of kindness and firmness that earned him the respect and affection of countless students. Tate played a crucial role in the peaceful integration of the university in 1961, and less than a decade later his presence at student antiwar demonstrations helped prevent the violence that occurred on many other campuses. Today the university is simply too large for an individual to exercise so great a personal influence on so many students. The college tradition, however, has been enriched by the presence of vivid personalities like "Uncle Tom" Reed and Dean Tate—campus characters in the best sense of the term.

Stegeman Hall · Clark Howell Hall

1943 · 1937

Stegeman Hall

To the west of the Tate Center, facing Lumpkin Street, is Stegeman Hall, named for Herman J. Stegeman, football coach and dean of men in the 1920s. Constructed during World War II for the U.S. Navy's preflight cadets, it contains a swimming pool, a gymnasium, and related facilities. The addition at the east end of Stegeman Hall serves as headquarters for the Public Safety Division, better known as the campus police.

For visitors who wish to see the dormitories built in the 1960s to house the fast-growing student population, Stegeman is a convenient point of departure. These buildings, which look very much like modern dormitories on other campuses, are to the southwest of Stegeman, along Baxter and Lumpkin Streets. On the left side of Baxter, the first is **Lipscomb Hall** (1961), named in honor of Andrew A. Lipscomb, the seventh president (or chancellor) of the university. **Mell Hall** (1961) was named for Chancellor Patrick Hues Mell (1878–88). **Bolton Dining Hall** (1963) honors J. D. Bolton, former treasurer of the university. The large dormitory next to Bolton is **Creswell Hall** (1963), named for Mary E. Creswell. Creswell, the first woman to receive the A.B. from the university, was dean of home economics from 1918 to 1945. **Russell Hall** (1967) was named for the late Senator Richard B. Russell, class of 1918. At the top of the hill is **Brumby Hall** (1966), named for Anne Brumby, second dean of women, who struggled in the 1920s to secure adequate housing for women students.

On the right side of Lumpkin Street is **Hill Hall** (1961), named for Walter B. Hill, chancellor of the university at

44

the turn of the century. Next to Hill is **Legion Pool**, the university's outdoor swimming pool, which is open to students, faculty, and their guests during spring and summer quarters. On the left, across Lumpkin Street, is Clark Howell Hall, originally a dormitory but now a center for student testing, career planning, and job placement. Howell (class of 1883) was a prominent Georgia politician and editor. Farther south on Lumpkin on the right are **Church Hall** (1961), named for Alonzo Church, president of the university from 1829 to 1859; and **Boggs Hall** (1961), named for William E. Boggs, who was president from 1888 to 1899. **Oglethorpe House**, the last dormitory on the right, was built privately in 1963 and purchased by the university in 1979. It was named for General James Oglethorpe, founder of the colony of Georgia. One

section of this relatively plush dormitory is reserved for women varsity athletes. Directly across Lumpkin Street is **Myers Hall** (1954); Jennie Belle Myers was a beloved housemother at the university for many years. (See the South Campus map for Church, Boggs, Oglethorpe, and Myers halls.) Farther south on Lumpkin Street, on the right, are most of the campus ministries; on the left are the South Campus Parking Deck and several buildings that we will visit later in the tour: the Georgia Center for Continuing Education, the Agricultural Extension Building, the football practice field, the track, and Butts-Mehre Heritage Hall, where our tour will eventually end.

We now retrace our steps to the eastern end of the parking lot behind the Tate Center, where we find the main entrance to Sanford Stadium.

Clark Howell Hall

Sanford Stadium

1929

For two decades after football arrived at the University of Georgia in 1892, games were played on a rough field behind New College. In 1911 a more formal field with a roofed wooden grandstand was constructed on the present site of Stegeman Hall. The football team shared the new stadium with several other sports, and intramural games also took place there.

By the 1920s a larger facility was needed. The logical site was a wooded valley separating the north and south campuses. Convict laborers diverted Tanyard Branch, which ran through the ravine, and sealed it in a concrete tunnel. Concrete stands seating thirty-three thousand were built along the north and south side, with the south stands over the creek; the east and west ends remained open. In the inaugural game on October 12, 1929, the Georgia Bulldogs defeated the Yale Bulldogs 17–0.

Sanford Stadium grew along with Georgia's football fortunes. An upper tier of seats constructed in 1967 increased capacity to almost sixty thousand. In 1981 the east end of the stadium was enclosed to increase seating to eighty-two thousand, and lights were added in 1982.

The stadium was named in honor of Steadman V. Sanford, a graduate of Mercer who came to the university in 1903 to teach English. During his forty-two years on the faculty, he held almost every administrative position imaginable. He headed the School of Journalism, chaired the faculty athletic committee, served as dean of the college and president of the university, and finally became chancellor of the University System of Georgia.

Over the years dramatic football games have been played "between the hedges," and many stars have performed. Frank Sinkwich won the Heisman Trophy in 1942, and superstar Charles Trippi led victorious squads later in the 1940s. Francis Tarkenton passed and ran his team to winning seasons in 1959 and 1960. Freshman sensation Herschel Walker led the Bulldogs to a national championship in 1980 and won the Heisman Trophy in 1982. Equally impressive is the quarter-century coaching career of Vince Dooley, who followed in the footsteps of two other great coaches, Harry Mehre and Wally Butts (see p. 78). At the time of his retirement from coaching in 1988, Dooley had established a remarkable record of 201 wins, 77 losses, and 10 ties.

At the west end of Sanford Stadium, near the bust of Sanford, is the burial place of the bulldogs who have been the mascots of the football team.

South Campus

South Campus

54. Oglethorpe House
55. Myers Hall
56. Dawson Hall
57. Soule Hall
58. Rutherford Hall
59. Mary Lyndon Hall
60. Physics Building
61. Geography-Geology-Speech Building
62. Chemistry Building
63. Biological Sciences Building
64. Livestock-Poultry Building
65. Food Science Building
66. Lumpkin House
67. Conner Hall
68. Barrow Hall
69. Physical Plant Building
70. Boyd Graduate Studies Center and Science Library
71. Hardman Hall
72. Electronics Shop
73. Women's Physical Education Building
74. Ecology Building
75. Pharmacy Building
76. Snelling Hall
77. Forest Resources Building
78. U.S.D.A. Forest Service Complex
79. Dairy Science Building
80. Biotechnology Center
81. Aderhold Hall
82. Tucker Hall
83. Parking Services Building
84. Miller Plant Sciences Building
85. College of Veterinary Medicine
86. Industrial Arts Building
87. Driftmier Engineering Center
88. McWhorter Hall
89. Henry Feild Stadium
90. Indoor Tennis Courts
91. Collegiate Tennis Hall of Fame
92. McPhaul Child and Family Development Center
93. Home Management Houses
94. Georgia Center for Continuing Education
95. South Campus Parking Deck
96. The Coliseum
97. Hoke Smith Annex
98. Hoke Smith Building
99. Alumni House
100. Football Practice Field
101. Varsity Track
102. Foley Field
103. Butts-Mehre Heritage Hall

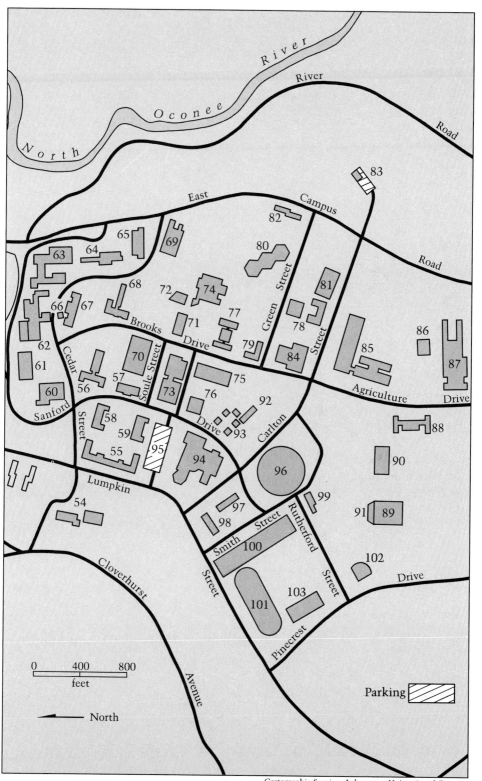

Dawson Hall

1932

To reach the south campus, the visitor walks along Sanford Drive, over the Jim L. Gillis, Sr., Bridge (1963). From the bridge one can look down into Sanford Stadium on the left. The route then follows Sanford Drive as it curves to the right and back to the left. The tour of south campus begins at the intersection of Sanford Drive and Cedar Street.

On the southeastern corner of the intersection stands Dawson Hall, named for Dr. William Terrell Dawson, who willed a sizeable fortune to the College of Agriculture in the 1920s. Dawson is the main building of the College of Home Economics.

The home economics program was established at the university in 1918, when women were admitted as undergraduates. For many years it occupied spare space in four different buildings on the south campus. When Dawson Hall was completed in 1932, the entire building was given over to the flourishing School of Home Economics. In 1984 a large eastern or rear annex, completed in 1971, was named in honor of Mary Spiers, dean of the school for many years. In 1982 an impressive Doric entrance was added to the west side of the original building, facing Sanford Drive.

Until recent years, almost all home economics majors were women. Now, as American society changes, men make up approximately 15 percent of the total enrollment.

Soule Hall

1920

The building beyond Dawson Hall on Sanford Drive is Soule Hall, the first women's dormitory on campus. Women gained admittance to the university as undergraduates in 1918, and Soule, which the male students called "the co-ed barn," was ready for occupancy in 1920. Relatively small and quiet, centrally located, it remains one of the most popular women's dormitories.

Soule Hall is named for Andrew M. Soule, who came to Georgia in 1907 to invigorate the agricultural program. Although agriculture had been a part of the university ever since it became a land-grant college in 1872, the program had generally been neglected. Soule was energetic, able, and not overly tactful. He sometimes seemed like the proverbial bull in the china shop to his colleagues on the old, traditional north campus, but he accom-plished a great deal during his quarter century of leadership. Soule was the father of the modern College of Agriculture and, in a sense, of today's whole bustling south campus of science and technology.

West of Soule Hall, across Sanford Drive, stands **Rutherford Hall** (1939), also a women's dormitory. It was named in honor of Mildred Lewis Rutherford, a noted author and educator. South of Rutherford is the graduate women's dormitory, **Mary Lyndon Hall** (1936), named for the first dean of women at the university. All three of these dormitories housed navy pre-flight cadets during World War II. At the west end of the quadrangle is Myers Hall, previously mentioned as one of the women's dormitories on Lumpkin Street.

The Science Center

1959–60

Physics Building

From the time of Josiah Meigs in the early nineteenth century, the university has shown an interest in the sciences. Scientific and technological training received greater emphasis after the university became a land-grant institution in 1872, though the trend was erratic and often strongly opposed. The real growth of the sciences at Georgia dates from 1957, when the Soviet Union launched the Sputnik satellite. The immediate result of the Soviet success was the series of buildings that line the north side of Cedar Street east of the intersection with Sanford Drive.

The six buildings, which form an arc just south of Sanford Stadium, were completed in 1960 and are known collectively as the Science Center. From west to east are the **Physics Building** with a 1969 addi-

tion, the **Geography-Geology-Speech Building**, the **Chemistry Building** with a 1971 annex, the **Biological Sciences Building** with a 1972 addition, the **Livestock-Poultry Building**, and the **Food Science Building**.

The Physics Building houses a telescope under a dome that is visible from the street. The telescope is a useful teaching tool, but its use in advanced research is limited by the glare and pollution of the Athens metropolitan area. The building also contains laser laboratories and a Van de Graff accelerator, located in restricted areas. In the lobbies of the Geography-Geology-Speech Building are displays of rocks, minerals, fossils, and maps, which visitors are welcome to examine.

From Field Street visitors can enter the west end of the Chemistry Building annex and observe the nuclear magnetic resonance facility at the end of the hall on the first floor. Here instruments determine the chemical structures of molecules. On the first floor of the Food Science Building visitors can see the pilot plant facilities, which demonstrate canning, dehydrating, smoking, packaging, and other techniques for handling food.

Geography-Geology-Speech Building

Chemistry Building

Biological Sciences Building

Livestock-Poultry Building

Food Science Building

Lumpkin House

1844

In the nineteenth century the future south campus was rolling residential and farm land unaffected by the small college to the north across Tanyard Branch. On a hill overlooking the creek was the Lumpkin House, the home of Wilson Lumpkin, the governor who removed the Cherokees from Georgia in the 1830s. In 1907 the Lumpkin family gave the house and several acres to the university, and the south campus began to take shape around it.

Lumpkin House, also called the "Rock House," is directly across from the Science Center, in a prime location close to the center of south campus. It was clear almost from the beginning that the old house stood in the way of progress; and the university would surely have demolished it,

had it not been for a peculiar clause in the bequest. The deed clearly stated that the entire grant—house and land—would revert to the family if the house was destroyed or moved. Thus a two-story indigenous structure with walls two feet thick at the base remains in the middle of the modern south campus.

The university has never quite known what to do with the "Rock House." Over the years it has served as a dormitory, a classroom building, a library, and almost everything else imaginable. Today it is used by the Cooperative Extension Service of the College of Agriculture. Doubtless it will always remain where it is— unless the university wants the Lumpkin heirs to set up housekeeping in the Science Center.

Conner Hall

1908

Immediately to the south of Lumpkin House stands Conner Hall, which seems enormous in comparison. Known as Agricultural Hall when it was completed in 1909, the building was renamed in 1923 in honor of James J. Conner, a state legislator who had strongly supported agricultural education in Georgia. This Renaissance Revival structure housed the fast-growing State College of Agriculture and the Mechanic Arts. Under its aggressive president, Andrew M. Soule, the A & M College sometimes resembled an independent school, separated from the old university by more than just Tanyard Branch.

In 1932 the flourishing A & M College was renamed the College of Agriculture and was brought firmly under the administrative control of the university. Probably more than any other division of the university, the College of Agriculture now reaches out from its headquarters in Conner Hall to bring its expertise to the people of Georgia and indeed the world. The college has established agricultural experiment stations in various parts of the state, and it cooperates with the U.S. Department of Agriculture in sponsoring the Cooperative Extension Service, which provides educational programs in agriculture, home economics, and 4-H and youth development.

Early in the 1970s Conner Hall was extensively renovated. The exterior seems little different except for the modern tinted windows, but the interior has been rebuilt for greater efficiency. Elevators have replaced the original three-story staircase, and a new central heating and cooling system provides greater economy.

Turning south from Conner Hall, we now follow the original main south campus road, first called Agriculture Drive and now named in honor of D. W. Brooks (class of 1921), president of the Gold Kist Corporation and a generous benefactor of the university.

Barrow Hall

1916

In 1916 the Farm Mechanics Building and the Agricultural Engineering Building were joined to form Barrow Hall. The building, enlarged in 1936 and again in 1952, is still occupied by the College of Agriculture. It also provides space for the electron microscopy laboratory.

David C. Barrow, for whom Barrow Hall is named, entered the university in 1869. Expelled for a year for fighting with another student after a Demosthenian meeting, he graduated in 1874. After practicing law for a few years, Barrow returned to the university to teach mathematics and civil engineering. He became dean in 1898. When Chancellor Hill died in 1905, Barrow was appointed the twelfth chancellor (or president) of the university.

During Barrow's nineteen years as chancellor, enrollment soared from fewer than four hundred students to more than sixteen hundred. From his plain office in the Academic Building, Barrow carried on Hill's modernization and expansion program in spite of financial restrictions. "Uncle Dave" was much beloved by the students in an age when faculty and administrators knew the students personally and exercised almost unlimited parental authority on campus. Barrow retired in 1925 at the age of seventy-three.

Behind Barrow Hall, to the southeast, is the **Physical Plant Building**, which contains a museum of natural history, open to the public by appointment.

Boyd Graduate Studies Center and Science Library

1968

The Graduate Studies Center, the most expensive project undertaken during the building boom of the 1960s, is really two buildings connected by a second-story hallway. The eight-story Graduate Studies Center, facing the street, houses the Graduate School and other administrative offices, the Department of Mathematics, and, in the basement, one of the most sophisticated computer centers in the South. The smaller Science Library, the west side of the complex, is a specialized satellite of the Main Library on the north campus. The planned addition of several stories to the library will raise it to the height of the Graduate Studies Center and make room for the science books and journals that continue to pour in.

In 1972 the center was named for a native Georgian, George H. Boyd, who was head of biological sciences for many years. In 1943 Boyd became dean of the Graduate School. He played a large part in developing Georgia into a major research institution.

Hardman Hall · Women's Physical Education Building

1922 · 1928

Hardman Hall

The next building on the left is Hardman Hall, which originally housed the Department of Animal Science. After World War II the College of Veterinary Medicine occupied Hardman for a short time. The building was used for women's physical education classes in the 1960s, and today it houses the Aerospace Studies (Air Force ROTC) program. The building was named for Lamartine G. Hardman, a physician who was much interested in education and who served as governor from 1927 to 1931.

The small building behind Hardman is the **Electronics Shop**, which repairs and services all of the computers on campus.

Across the street from Hardman Hall is the Women's Physical Education Building, completed in 1928. In 1969 an addition was constructed on the west side of the building, and the available floor space was more than doubled. The building contains a swimming pool, a gymnasium, an auditorium, and many offices and classrooms.

Ecology Building

1974

To the southeast of Hardman Hall stands the low brick Ecology Building, completed in 1974. The Institute of Ecology supports multidisciplinary research in marine and freshwater ecology, thermal ecology, radiation ecology, population and community ecology, mineral cycling, tropical and temperate forests, old field dynamics, agroecosystems, granite outcrops, and swamps. Its service programs provide environmental assessments to government and industry, and the institute also offers short courses in ecology. The flourishing ecology program is largely the creation of Eugene P. Odum, who joined the university faculty in 1940 as a zoologist. Odum, a pioneer in the field of ecology, established the Institute of Ecology in 1961.

In 1977 an annex was built at the rear of the building. The addition houses two related but separate operations: the Institute of Natural Resources and the Marine Sciences Program. The Institute of Natural Resources is an interdisciplinary program that conducts research on applications of science to issues affecting natural-resource management and policy analyses. The Marine Sciences Program coordinates the Marine Institute on Sapelo Island, the Marine Extension Service, and the Georgia Sea Grant College Program.

Robert C. Wilson Pharmacy Building

1964

In 1903 the School of Pharmacy was established as part of Chancellor Hill's modernization program. For the first three decades of its existence, it occupied cramped quarters in the basement of Terrell Hall. The program moved to the second and third floors of New College in 1939, but this arrangement too soon became inadequate. Not until 1964 did the College of Pharmacy join the other major sciences on the south campus, where it is now housed in a modern three-story building that covers an area the size of a football field.

Robert C. Wilson, a native Georgian, was a pharmacist in Athens when he accepted an instructorship at the university in 1907. In 1917 he became the dean of the School of Pharmacy. By 1928 he had instituted a four-year program of study, one of the first in the nation, and he continued to build his program until his retirement in 1949. On his one-hundredth birthday in 1978, the new pharmacy building was named in his honor—a departure from the university's rule that no structure can be named for a living person. Wilson died in 1981 at the age of 103.

Behind the Pharmacy Building, to the west, are the university's **experimental gardens** maintained by the Department of Horticulture. Interested visitors will enjoy walking through the gardens to see the display of new varieties of annuals and perennials.

Snelling Hall

1940

From the north side of the Pharmacy Building, one can see Snelling Hall, half a block west on the corner of Sanford Drive and Green Street. It was one of the seventeen buildings constructed in the late 1930s by the Public Works Administration. It has served as a cafeteria since its completion in 1940. During World War II the U.S. Navy used it as a dining hall for the preflight cadets. The building was renovated in 1969, and a 1979 addition has helped it serve the growing numbers of students and faculty.

Charles M. Snelling, for whom the dining hall is named, graduated from the Virginia Military Institute in 1884 and came to Georgia to teach mathematics. He also commanded the cadet corps that every land-grant college was required to have. He became dean under Chancellor Barrow, whom he succeeded in 1926. Six years later he was appointed the first chancellor of the new University System of Georgia, which includes all public schools of higher education. Snelling retired in 1933.

Forest Resources Building

1938

Across Brooks Drive from the Pharmacy Building stands the home of the School of Forest Resources. The forestry program began on the north campus in 1906 with considerable support from the philanthropist George Foster Peabody. It soon moved to the south campus, but for many years it struggled along in temporary, cramped quarters—one of its small buildings was none too fondly known as the "dog house." In 1939 the school moved into a brick structure, another of the seventeen "classic PWA" buildings. The U.S. Navy took over the building during World War II. A large addition completed in 1968 more than doubled the available space.

Behind the Forest Resources Building to the southeast (across Green Street) are two U.S. Department of Agriculture **Forest Service buildings**, constructed in the early 1960s. The Forest Service works closely with the School of Forestry and other departments on the south campus.

Dairy Science Building

1939

Just south of the original Forest Resources Building is the similar Dairy Science Building. It contains classrooms, laboratories, and the creamery, where university students, faculty, and the general public can buy yogurt, milk, cheese, ice cream, and other dairy products. The rest of the dairy science facilities are housed in the larger Livestock-Poultry Building.

Biotechnology Center

At Green Street, on the south side of the Dairy Science Building, the tour briefly turns to the east. Under construction on the north side of Green Street, behind Dairy Science, is the Biotechnology Center. Here the university will concentrate many of its resources in a major commitment to biotechnology. For many years the university has supported a strong program of research in the biological sciences and in such fields as agriculture, forestry, veterinary medicine, and pharmacy. This emphasis is now complemented by research on the molecular level in the plant and animal sciences, genetics, microbiology, and biochemistry. In all of these fields, modern techniques of genetic research hold the promise of many new products of importance to industry and to Georgia's economy.

Focal points for the biotechnology program include the Center for Plant Cell and Molecular Biology, the Center for Biological Resource Recovery, the Center for Nitrogen Fixation and Metalloenzyme Studies, and the Complex Carbohydrate Research Center. These interdisciplinary centers have led to the development of a particularly strong core of researchers in plant molecular biology, fermentation research, enzyme studies, and complex carbohydrate chemistry.

Aderhold Hall · Tucker Hall

1971 · 1961

Aderhold Hall

Just across Green Street from the Biotechnology Center stands Aderhold Hall, completed in 1971. This seven-story structure contains offices and classrooms for the College of Education.

O. C. Aderhold, for whom the building is named, graduated from the university in the class of 1923. After earning a Ph.D. from Ohio State University, Aderhold returned to the university to teach rural and vocational education. In 1946 he became dean of the College of Education, and in 1950 he was chosen as the seventeenth president of the university. During the seventeen years of his presidency, enrollment grew from 6,300 to 16,200. In the later years of the Ader-

hold administration, the university began to gain recognition as a research institution.

Tucker Hall, beyond the Biotechnology Center on the north side of Green Street, houses the School of Social Work and several administrative offices of the College of Education. Constructed as a dormitory in 1961, the building is named in honor of Henry H. Tucker, president of the university from 1874 to 1878.

One block southeast of Tucker Hall on Carlton Street is the **Parking Services Building**. Visitors who need to park in areas not designated for visitor parking must obtain a temporary permit from Parking Services.

Miller Plant Sciences Building

1972

The large building on the southeast corner of Brooks Drive and Green Street houses the Departments of Agronomy, Botany, Horticulture, and Plant Pathology. It also provides space for the herbarium, a collection of dried Georgia plants, which is open to the public by appointment. Built in 1972, it is named for Professor Julian H. Miller, a professor of plant pathology from 1919 to 1958. Miller was chairman of the Division of Plant Pathology for a number of years and was one of the first university professors to gain national recognition for his research.

Veterinary Medicine · Driftmier Engineering Center

1949 · 1966

College of Veterinary Medicine

The College of Veterinary Medicine is located on the southeastern corner of Brooks Drive and Carlton Street. The program, originally established on south campus in 1915, was housed in Hardman Hall until 1932, when it was discontinued. Because of a growing need for veterinary skills in the Southeast, the program was reestablished immediately after World War II. To make room for a veterinary medicine building, a lake was drained and the surrounding campground was graded. The new building, which faces Brooks Drive, was completed in 1949. In 1973 an annex was constructed on the south side of the original building, and in 1979 a modern teaching hospital was completed on the north side of the complex.

Fred C. Davison, president of the university from 1967 to 1986, is an alumnus of the College of Veterinary Medicine (class of 1952). In 1964, Davison, who had also earned a Ph.D. in pathology and biochemistry from Iowa State University, returned to the college as dean. Three years later, at the age of thirty-seven, he became Georgia's eighteenth president. Davison's wife, Dianne, was one of the two women who received degrees from the college in 1952. Women now make up at least half of every graduating class.

South of the College of Veterinary Medicine is the **Industrial Arts Building** (1971) and the much larger Driftmier Engineering Center named for Rudolph H. Driftmier, former head of agricultural engineering. As supervising engineer, Driftmier directed the building boom of the 1930s on campus and throughout the entire state system of higher education. The Driftmier Engineering Center houses the Department of Agricultural Engineering.

McWhorter Hall

1967

Just south of the College of Veterinary Medicine, across Brooks Drive, stands McWhorter Hall, the men's athletic dormitory. Built in 1967, it was expanded and extensively renovated in 1987 and today is one of the best such facilities in the nation. McWhorter offers several amenities not seen in the other university dorms—a small chapel and a cafeteria that serves specially planned meals to about 160 athletes.

Robert McWhorter, for whom the dormitory was named, was a native Athenian and a member of a family whose sons and daughters have attended Georgia for generations. McWhorter entered the university in 1910, the year before the university constructed its first permanent football field. The stocky, speedy halfback became Georgia's first All-American and first member of the College Football Hall of Fame.

Henry Feild Stadium

1977

West of McWhorter Hall is Feild Stadium, named for the "little professor," the top player on the tennis teams of 1964–66, who died in an automobile accident in 1968. The stadium has three courts and, with the addition of temporary bleachers, can accommodate five thousand spectators. Next to it are six courts for women, four **indoor courts** (named for Lindsey Hopkins, class of 1929), and three more outdoor courts. For many years the NCAA tournament was held at Feild Stadium every spring, and the **Collegiate Tennis Hall of Fame** was built there in 1984.

The credit for building both a fine tennis program and excellent facilities belongs to Dan Magill, class of 1942, who coached the tennis team for over three decades. Traditionally tennis courts at Georgia were placed in out-of-the-way areas, only to be moved again when planners concluded that the level courts would make a good site for new construction. In the 1940s Magill and his teammates played on the north campus where the Psychology-Journalism Complex now stands. The teams of the 1950s played in a small stadium which was demolished to make way for the Science Center at the end of the decade. Six permanent courts were constructed on the present site in the 1960s, and the first match was played in Feild Stadium in 1977.

McPhaul Child and Family Development Center

1940

From McWhorter Hall and Feild Stadium we retrace our steps for a block, walking northward along Brooks Drive to the corner of Brooks and Carlton Street. There we turn left and walk westward, with the Coliseum as a landmark on the left. Facing the large parking lot across Carlton Street from the Coliseum stands the McPhaul Center, the university's laboratory school for preschool children.

In 1927 the Rockefeller Foundation gave the university funds for a nursery school, which is a part of the child development program of the College of Home Economics. Margaret McPhaul, for whom the center is named, directed it from 1937 until her retirement in 1961. The laboratory school moved to a new PWA building in 1940, and in 1971 a large addition in front allowed the program to expand.

Just west of the McPhaul Center are four **home management houses**, also part of the College of Home Economics. They were completed in 1939 with PWA funds. For many years, home economics students majoring in certain areas were required to live in one of these residences for one quarter. Several of the houses now contain administrative offices.

Georgia Center for Continuing Education

1957

At the corner of Lumpkin and Carlton streets is the Continuing Education complex, built in 1957 with a grant from the W. K. Kellogg Foundation and matching funds from the state. The five-story building contains meeting and classroom facilities, dining and banqueting areas, and rooms for overnight guests. The center offers residential conferences and short courses; on- and off-campus programs for credit, no credit, and teacher certification; audioconferences and teleconferences. It sponsors the Independent Study Program, operates a National Public Radio station, and houses television and film production facilities. The center's flourishing programs have served as a model for adult education programs in other states.

In 1984 the Kellogg Foundation pledged fifteen million dollars for new programs and construction, and the state committed another seven million to expand the original building. The additions have almost doubled the size of the building—the number of overnight rooms has increased from 144 to 201, for example—and the five-tier **South Campus Parking Deck**, which is open to the general public, has been constructed behind the complex. When the construction is completed, Georgia will have the largest university-based continuing education center in the world.

The Coliseum · Hoke Smith Building

1964 · 1937

The Coliseum

Until the completion of the Coliseum in 1964, Georgia had fielded mediocre basketball teams that were handicapped by inadequate facilities. The Coliseum, across Carlton Street from the Continuing Education Center, provides a first-rate environment for first-rate teams, women's as well as men's.

The Coliseum, however, is much more than a basketball arena. It houses offices for the coaching staffs of all sports except football, which has moved to the new Butts-Mehre Heritage Hall. The Coliseum also hosts agricultural shows, concerts, commencements, rodeos, and virtually any other activity requiring 11,200 seats.

Just west of the Coliseum lies the **Hoke Smith Annex** (1940), originally a dormitory, and the Agricultural Extension Building, recently renamed the Hoke Smith Building. Smith was governor of Georgia from 1907 to 1909 and again in 1911. As a United States senator in 1914, he cosponsored the Smith-Lever Act, which provided federal funds for agricultural extension work.

Alumni House

1943

Walking around to the south side of the Coliseum, we see Alumni House, originally a field house constructed by the navy during World War II. The naval preflight program, stressing physical fitness and combativeness, built a track and four football fields for training sessions. The field house was designed to support these activities. At the end of the war the navy left, and the field house served Georgia's own athletic program until the Coliseum was completed in 1964. For a while it housed experimental animals. In 1969 it became the headquarters of the Alumni Society and the Office of Alumni Relations, which tries to keep up with the university's living alumni, who numbered 145,000 in 1987.

Directly in front of the Alumni House is the **football practice field**, which allows the team to become accustomed to playing on artificial turf. Beyond the practice field is the new **varsity track**. Behind the track is the lighted **baseball field** named for Frank Foley, who played for Georgia in the early 1900s and later became a member of the Board of Regents.

Butts-Mehre Heritage Hall

1987

At the southern edge of the main campus, on the corner of Rutherford Street and Pinecrest Drive, is a new campus landmark: Butts-Mehre Heritage Hall, the headquarters of the athletic program. In keeping with the tradition of mixing architectural styles on campus, this glass-domed structure of pink and black marble is unique. The first floor contains modern locker and training facilities for the football team; the second, administrative offices; the third, a museum of Georgia football history, the athletic ticket office, and the sports information department; and the fourth, space for more offices and for the headquarters of the athletic boosters' organization, the Georgia Bulldog Club.

Built by the independent Athletic Association, Heritage Hall honors two of Georgia's greatest football coaches, Wallace Butts and Harry Mehre. Mehre, a graduate of Notre Dame, came to Georgia in 1924 as line coach. He became head coach in 1928, and during the next ten years his teams won 59 games, lost 34, and tied 6. Wally Butts, a Mercer University alumnus who was head coach at Georgia from 1939 to 1960, compiled a 140-86-9 record. Butts's 1942 team, led by Charlie Trippi and Frank Sinkwich, won the Rose Bowl and claimed the national title. The 1946 team, with Trippi as captain, was undefeated.

A Driving Tour

Much of the university campus is not within convenient walking distance of the main north and south campuses. Visitors with a car and an hour or two to spare may therefore choose to follow a driving tour of the outlying areas. This route, like the route of the walking tour, takes the visitor to both new and old parts of the university.

Driving Tour

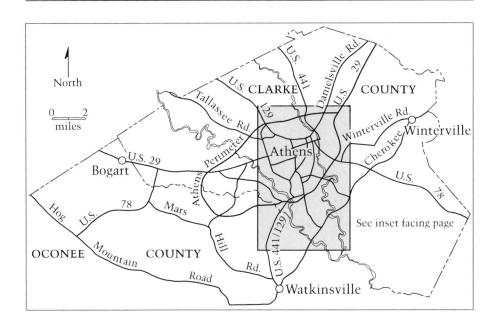

1. University Village
2. Family Housing Office
3. Lake Herrick
4. Oconee Forest Park
5. Four Towers
6. Riverbend Research Laboratories
7. Complex Carbohydrate Research Center
8. Georgia Retardation Center
9. Russell Agricultural Research Center
10. U.S. Environmental Protection Agency Research Laboratory
11. Poultry Disease Research Center
12. Soil Testing and Plant Analysis Laboratory
13. University Golf Course
14. State Botanical Garden of Georgia
15. White Hall Mansion
16. Lucy Cobb Institute
17. Seney-Stovall Chapel
18. President's House
19. Lumpkin House
20. Coordinate Campus

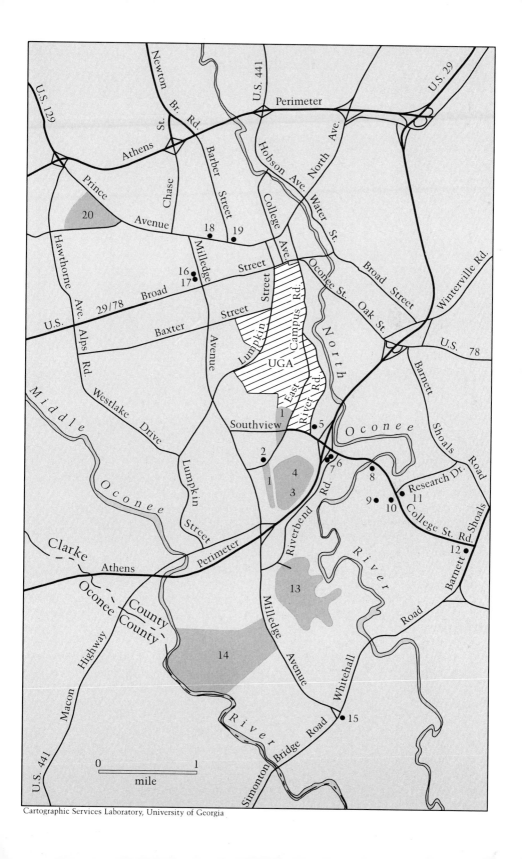

University Village

1964

The driving tour begins at the intersection of Southview/College Station Road and East Campus Road, slightly over four-tenths mile south of Aderhold Hall. University Village, on the northwest and southwest corners of the intersection, is the university's first permanent apartment complex for married students.

Until the mid-twentieth century few married students enrolled at the university. After World War II the GI Bill brought a great many veterans to campus, not only at Georgia but throughout the country. Most of these veterans were older than the usual age, and many were married. Like other large universities, Georgia housed the veterans and their families in all kinds of temporary quarters.

Old military barracks were a favorite expedient—not fancy but inexpensive.

Although the flood of veterans entering college began to subside in the 1950s, the university's growing graduate and professional schools continued to attract older students, many of whom were married. In 1964 the university, recognizing that the composition of the student body had changed permanently, opened the first 105 units of University Village, and additional units were built in 1966. Just south of University Village, on East Campus Road, is the **Family Housing Office** (1970). Another large area of married housing was constructed on the opposite side of East Campus Road in 1972.

College Station Road Facilities

Lake Herrick

We now drive east from University Village on College Station Road, crossing the railroad tracks. On the right are the university's intramural athletic fields and a new pavilion overlooking **Lake Herrick**, which was named for Allyn M. Herrick, former dean of the School of Forest Resources. South of the lake is the **Oconee Forest Park**, part of the School of Forest Resources. The park furnishes wonderful walking trails. On the left of College Station Road are dairy and poultry research facilities, including the **Four Towers** barn complex (1937).

Driving east on College Station Road for about half a mile, we pass the **Riverbend Research Laboratories** (1974) and the new **Complex Carbohydrate Research Center** (1989), on the right just before we cross the

Oconee River. The **Automotive Center**, which operates the fleet of campus buses, is also located here. Just beyond the river on the right stands the Athens Unit of the **Georgia Retardation Center** (1969), a state agency affiliated with the university.

A little farther on the right stands the U.S. Department of Agriculture's **Richard B. Russell Agricultural Research Center** (1970) and the **U.S. Environmental Protection Agency Research Laboratory** (1966), both of which work closely with various scientific and technical departments on the south campus. The cluster of low buildings across College Station Road on the left is the **Poultry Disease Research Center** (1953). On the right at the end of College Station Road is the **Soil Testing and Plant Analysis Laboratory** of the College of Agriculture Cooperative Extension Service.

Four Towers

Poultry Disease Research Center

Soil Testing and Plant Analysis Laboratory

State Botanical Garden of Georgia

1969

Callaway Building

We now retrace the route back across the railroad tracks, where we turn left on East Campus Drive. At the intersection of East Campus Drive and Milledge Avenue, a little more than half a mile from the railroad crossing, we turn left again and drive out Milledge toward Whitehall. On the left, three-tenths mile past the bridges that cross over Milledge, is Riverbend Road leading to the university's fine and demanding eighteen-hole **golf course,** which is often open to the public on a first-come, first-served basis. A little more than half a mile farther, on the right, is the entrance to the State Botanical Garden of Georgia, which is open to the public.

In 1831 the university established a botanical garden near the campus. The garden was a source of pride to the college, but it eventually proved

too expensive to maintain, and in 1856 the college was forced to sell it. The funds received from the sale paid for the Arch and the iron fence erected in front of north campus just before the Civil War.

Over a century later, in the late 1960s, the university established a large new garden, which has received generous support from the Callaway Foundation of LaGrange, Georgia. The three-hundred-acre garden functions as a living plant library and offers everything from nature trails over diverse terrain to facilities for formal receptions. The rose garden is well worth seeing, and in the spring wildflowers bloom in abundance along the paths that lead to the river. There are two main buildings: the **Callaway Building**, completed in 1975, and the much larger, glass-encased **Visitor**

Visitor Center/Conservatory

Interior, Visitor Center/Conservatory

Center/Conservatory, opened in 1985. The Conservatory houses tropical and semitropical plants and is open to the public daily until 4:30. The Botanical Garden, which serves as an outdoor laboratory for university classes and offers short courses to the general public, is a model for such projects at other schools across the nation.

White Hall Mansion

1892

Farther south on Milledge Avenue are fields and livestock barns belonging to the College of Agriculture. The cows and sheep that graze in fenced pastures on both sides of the road are part of the college's research programs.

At the end of Milledge Avenue is the mill village of Whitehall and a large house that serves as a reception center for the School of Forest Resources. The mansion, known as White Hall, was designed by Professor Charles M. Strahan, who mixed Victorian and Gothic styles. It was completed in 1892 for John Richards White, the owner of the nearby mill. In the 1970s the mansion was renovated and placed on the National Register of Historic Places. Toward the back of the estate is a more informal meeting place, called **Flinchum's Phoenix** in honor of the graduate student who built it.

Lucy Cobb Institute

1858

Lucy Cobb Institute

From White Hall we follow Milledge Avenue over three miles back into the center of Athens. Past Five Points (the intersection of Milledge and Lumpkin), on both sides of Milledge, are many of the fraternity and sorority houses that play a large role in the social life of university undergraduate students. Although Milledge Avenue is technically "off campus," it is very much a part of the university, one of the links between the college and the city that surrounds it. By restoring and maintaining antebellum houses, several of the Greek-letter organizations have helped preserve a section of old Athens.

On the west side of Milledge Avenue, just north of Broad Street, is the Lucy Cobb Institute. In 1858 Thomas R. R. Cobb (class of 1841), one of the founders of the Law School, helped establish a high school for young

ladies from prominent local families. The school was named for Cobb's daughter, who had recently died of scarlet fever. Over the years Lucy Cobb became a well-known girls' preparatory school. Unfortunately, the school did not survive the depression.

The university, which took over the campus in 1931, used the main building as a women's dormitory for many years. The structure gradually deteriorated, and the fourth floor was removed in 1954. Eventually the buildings, which were too far from the main campus to make extensive repair work worthwhile, were used mainly for storage. In 1984 the federal government appropriated three million dollars to renovate the building. When the work is completed, Lucy Cobb will house the Carl Vinson Institute of Government.

Next to the main building is the

Seney-Stovall Chapel, constructed in 1885 as part of the Lucy Cobb Institute. The university used the building as a theater until the Fine Arts Building was completed in 1941. Like the main building, the chapel was then allowed to fall into disrepair. In 1981 a combination of federal, university, and private funds financed the renovation of the exterior of the building.

Seney-Stovall Chapel

President's House

1856

At the end of Milledge Avenue, the tour turns right on Prince Avenue and proceeds two-tenths of a mile. On the left is the President's House, surrounded by a white picket fence. This striking Greek revival mansion was built in 1856 by John T. Grant, a university alumnus who prospered constructing railroads. After the Civil War, Benjamin H. Hill, a prominent politician, lived there. Later the Athens industrialist John White acquired it.

By the time of World War II the house had fallen into disrepair. In 1949 the W. C. Bradley Foundation presented it to the university, which meticulously restored the building and grounds as a home and a reception center for the president. The antebellum house, with its beautiful gardens, is a fitting symbol for one of the nation's oldest state universities.

Two-tenths of a mile farther, on the same side of the street, is the **Lumpkin House**, a restored antebellum mansion which was originally the home of Joseph Henry Lumpkin, a distinguished Georgia jurist who helped establish the Law School in 1859. Appropriately, the house now contains the university's Institute of Continuing Legal Education. Lumpkin Street is also named for Joseph Henry Lumpkin.

The Coordinate Campus

Winnie Davis Hall

A little more than a mile in the opposite direction on Prince Avenue is Normaltown, where the visitor may see the campus of what was formerly the State Normal School, established in 1891 on the north side of Athens, at a site that had belonged to the university for several decades. Before the Civil War, Chancellor Lipscomb planned to move the freshman and sophomore classes to this location, but so much opposition arose among the students that the original building, informally known as Rock College (1862), was renamed University High School and served as a prep school. After the war it housed Confederate veterans who were not ready for college work.

When Georgia became a land-grant college in 1872, Rock College and the surrounding area were used as an experimental farm. When the State Normal School took over the campus, the area became known as Normaltown. Rock College was renamed Gilmer Hall, and seven new buildings were constructed for the Normal School.

In 1933, when Governor Richard B. Russell established a unified system of public higher education in Georgia, the campus became the Coordinate College of the university. All freshman and sophomore women were housed there. Although young women were no more enthusiastic about this arrangement than the young men had been back in 1859, the Coordinate Campus remained a part of the university for twenty years.

In 1954 the Navy Supply Corps bought the property for the Supply Corps School. The navy demolished Gilmer Hall and constructed many buildings and facilities. Still, several of the old Normal School–Coordinate Campus buildings remain, a reminder of the university's presence in Normaltown. The most prominent of these is **Winnie Davis Hall** (1902), now the main administration building. Named for Jefferson Davis's daughter, it served as a dormitory for the State Normal School and, from 1933 to 1954, as a women's dormitory on the Coordinate Campus. West of Winnie Davis Hall is the old **Carnegie Library** (1910), now a museum of the history of the Supply Corps School. It is open Monday through Friday from 8 A.M. to 4:30 P.M.

Carnegie Library

Photograph Credits

All photographs in this book were taken by Walter P. Montgomery, University of Georgia Office of Public Information, with the exception of the following:

Soule Hall, Lumpkin House, and Barrow Hall (photographs by Chuck Moore)

Meigs Hall and George Peabody Hall (photographs by Dennis O'Kain, University Archives)

University Village, Georgia Center for Continuing Education, and McPhaul Child and Family Development Center (photographs by Michael L. Barrett, Georgia Center for Continuing Education)

Henry Feild Stadium, McWhorter Hall, and Sanford Stadium (courtesy of Athletic Association)

The Coliseum (photograph by Bob Simonton, Athletic Association)

Butts-Mehre Heritage Hall (photograph by Thom White, Athletic Association)

Winnie Davis Hall and Carnegie Library (photographs by Marion Doolittle, Navy Supply Corps School)

Brooks Hall (courtesy of College of Business Administration)

College of Veterinary Medicine (photograph by Susan Snyder, College of Veterinary Medicine)

Index